WHAT WILL I BE FROM A TO Z

LAURA W CarteR & ANNA DohERty

Published by Familius LLC, www.familius.com
PO Box 1130, Sanger, CA 93657

Familius books are available at special discounts for bulk purchases, whether
for sales promotions or for family or corporate use. For more information,
contact Familius Sales at orders@familius.com.

Library of Congress Control Number: 2025930352

Print ISBN 9781641709620
Ebook ISBN 9798893965148

Printed in China

Edited by Laurie Duersch
Cover design by Anna Doherty
Book design by Brooke Jorden

10 9 8 7 6 5 4 3 2 1

First Edition

I may be small, but I dream big about what I might be.
My future's bright, no end in sight, with options A to Z.

I want to be an ASTRONAUT,
who learns about the stars.
Earth's gravity won't weigh on me
when traveling to Mars.

I want to be a BIOLOGIST
and learn about the Earth.
From sky to sea and in between,
I'll fight to prove its worth.

I want to be a CHEMIST,
with my periodic chart
of solid, gas, and liquid mass.
I'll learn them all by heart.

I want to be a DESIGNER of graphics large and small.
From signs to bags and books to tags, I'll print my work on all.

I want to be an ENGINEER,
to draft and then create.
I'll take apart, and then restart,
inventions that are great.

I want to be a FORECASTER and track the atmosphere.

From sun to rain and hurricanes, both pleasant and severe.

I want to be a GEOLOGIST
and study sediment lines
beneath the dust and Earth's thick crust,
from mountain peaks to mines.

I want to be a HORTICULTURIST
and give plants what they need.
I'll water right and give them light
to grow them up from seed.

I want to be an INTERNIST
and treat what makes you ill.
I'll cure your tum, your heart, and bum
with medicine and skill.

I want to be a JAVA DEVELOPER and type out complex code.
I'll write software, and then I'll share, for people to download.

I want to be a KINESIOLOGIST
and study how we move.

I want to be a LASER TECH
and bend bright beams of light.
I'll draw, design, and then align
to help restore your sight.

We will not sit—I'll get you fit!
And help your health improve.

I want to be a MUSICIAN
and play guitar and sing.
My music notes will swell and float,
from jazz to rock to swing.

I want to be a NEUROLOGIST
and study spines and brains.
I'll scrutinize your MRIs
and treat your migraine pains.

I want to be an ONCOLOGIST
and lead the cancer fight.
I'll scan your chest and do my best
to make sure you're all right.

I want to be a PHOTOGRAPHER
of mountains, lakes, and skies.

I'll capture caves and birds and waves and flitting butterflies.

I want to be a QUANTUM PHYSICIST
and study molecules.
Atomic bits and nuclear splits,
I'll test the quantum rules.

I want to be a ROBOT TECH
and build one piece by piece.
Its wires, bolts, and steady volts
will be a masterpiece.

I want to be a SCREENWRITER
and write grand movie scenes.
You'll laugh and cry and yelp and sigh
while watching on your screens.

I want to be a school TEACHER
and help kids learn to think.
From math and arts to science charts,
I'll teach them link by link.

I want to be an URBAN PLANNER
for cities large and small.
From building sites to traffic lights,
I'll manage urban sprawl.

I want to be a VETERINARIAN and cure your pets, of course.
Your cats and dogs and birds and hogs—I'll even treat your horse.

I want to be a WELDER,
who helps build people's dreams.
With torch in hand, I'll make things grand,
connecting metal beams.

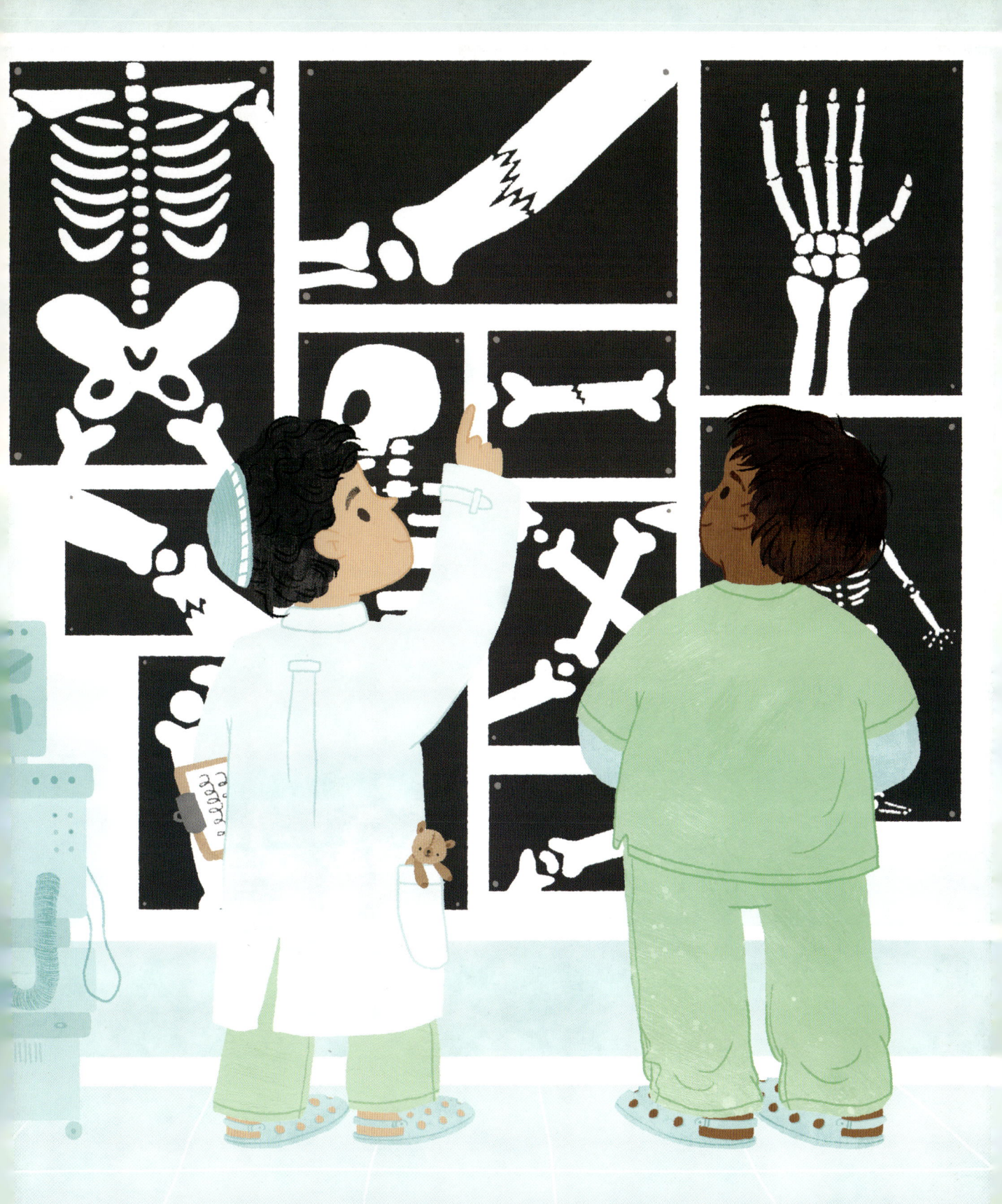

I want to be an X-RAY TECH and photograph your bones.
You'll hold real still, I'll use my skill to read the black/white tones.

I want to be a YOGA INSTRUCTOR
and help you meditate.

I want to be a ZOOLOGIST, for creatures small and grand.
I'll help you see why we should be protecting life on land.

You'll twist and bend,
and then extend.
Your balance will be great.

So what will I decide to be,
with options in the thousands?
I don't know yet, but this I'll bet:
I promise I'll move mountains.

Career Research Questions

Do you want to learn more about one of the jobs mentioned in this book? Here are some questions to help you get started.

First, let's pick a job.
1. What do I want to be when I grow up? (or What will I be, from A to Z?)
2. What makes me interested in this job?
3. Why do I think I'd be good at this job?

Next, let's prepare for the job.
4. What should I study so I can be good at this job?
5. Do I need to go to college to learn how to do this job?
6. What tools would I need to learn how to use for this job?

Finally, let's do the job!
7. What would I do each day if I took this job?
8. Who would I help if I took this job?
9. What would I wear to work if I took this job?